STING AND NEST

Poems

Praise for *Sting and Nest*

In *Sting and Nest*, Barbara Rockman has vividly "memorize[d] every possible loss," stretching from childhood to motherhood to the loss of one's parents. Simultaneously, these poems are a well-crafted, evocative "Search & Rescue" of experience located in the interior of family life, that "City of Heart." Here, the bed is "busy with blue gasps," Buddha is present in the form of a dog, and one "traffics in the imperfect," all the while asking, "*Can you love too much?*" This debut collection is wonderfully, acutely worded and felt.

—Rebecca Seiferle, Lannan fellowship recipient,
author of *The Ripped-Out Seam* and *Wild Tongue*

Barbara Rockman's *Sting and Nest* is a collection of poetry whose attention to all of the most important elements of craft is consistently strong and enduring. This is combined with a heightened sense of brevity that allows the poet to shape and hone the rigmarole of our domestic lives into tightly wound and powerfully satisfying poems.

—Bruce Weigl, winner of the
Academy of American Poets Prize,
author of *Song of Napalm* and *The Circle of Hanh*

STING AND NEST

Poems

Barbara Rockman

SANTA FE

Sunstone books may be purchased for educational, business, or sales promotional use.
For information please write: Special Markets Department, Sunstone Press,
P.O. Box 2321, Santa Fe, New Mexico 87504-2321.

Book and Cover design ∼ Vicki Ahl
Body typeface ∼ Adobe Garamond Pro
Printed on acid free paper

Library of Congress Cataloging-in-Publication Data

Rockman, Barbara, 1949-
  Sting and nest : poems / by Barbara Rockman.
       p. cm.
  ISBN 978-0-86534-807-3 (pbk. : alk. paper)
  I. Title.
  PS3618.O35447S75 2011
  811'.6--dc22
                        2011003717

Published in

WWW.SUNSTONEPRESS.COM
SUNSTONE PRESS / POST OFFICE BOX 2321 / SANTA FE, NM 87504-2321 /USA
(505) 988-4418 / ORDERS ONLY (800) 243-5644 / FAX (505) 988-1025

To Beth, Elana, and Rick,
for inspiration and love.

In memory of my parents,
Mary and Herbert Glodt.

CONTENTS

III

IV

ACKNOWLEDGMENTS

Many of these poems first appeared, sometimes in slightly different versions, in the following journals and anthologies:

California Quarterly; *Calyx, A Journal of Art and Literature by Women*; *The Cape Rock*; *Chaffin Journal*; *The Comstock Review*; *Concho River Review*; *Cradle Songs: Anthology of Motherhood* (Quill and Parchment Press); *damselfly press*; *descant*; *Eclipse*; *Harwood Anthology* (Old School Books); *Kalliope*; *Karamu*; *Lavanderia: A Mixed Load of Women, Wash and Word* (City Works Press); *Looking Back to Place* (Old School Books); *The MacGuffin*; *Manzanita Quarterly*; *Monadnock Writers Anthology*; *Pearl*; *Persimmon Tree*; *Poetica*; *Quiddity*; *Red Rock Review*; *The Return of the River* (Sunstone Press); *Santa Clara Review*; *Santa Fe Literary Review*; *Sanskrit*; *Schuykill Valley Journal*; *Southern Humanities Review*; *Sow's Ear Poetry Review*; *Spoon River Poetry Review*; *Tiger's Eye Journal*; *Voices of New Mexico* (Rio Grande Books); *Women Becoming Poems: An Anthology of Women's Voices* (Cinabar Press)

∾

Special thanks are due to Robyn Covelli-Hunt, Sheila Cowing, Wayne Lee, and Donald Levering, fellow poets who have been careful readers of many of these poems. I am indebted to Bruce Weigl and Dana Levin, who helped shape my poems into a book. Thank you to Michael Scofield for his encouragement, and to Richard Lehnert for his editing expertise. For my teachers at Vermont College of Fine Arts, who set me on the path, and for my students, who offer endless inspiration and joy, I am most grateful.

THOUGHTS ON MAKING A BOOK

I watch comings and goings in the gray nest above the entrance to our house as I watched the busy lives of wasps as a child. These insects have created a home symmetrically intricate and yet elegantly practical in its ability to endure. I witness the wasps' constant buzz and wariness. I am intrigued by the harmony of clustered cells in which the young are nurtured and protected against threat and hunger. I am captivated by the hovering swarm, the papery walls constructed by instinct, and the possibility of being stung.

∾

A first book of poems is a stumbling into the light. It is clearing one's throat and speaking at risk. It is a self-introduction. It is a flexing of tone and timbre, theme and style. It is a public offering of a private life. It is finding one's footing and inching toward one's vision. It is a revelation of obsession.

∾

When I was thirteen, my parents took me to a walnut-paneled hall on the campus of Williams College to hear Robert Frost read his poems. I had already fallen for this man who understood the pastures, sunsets, woods, and rhythms of my solitary wanderings in the landscape we shared. Hearing his voice secured my devotion. Although I would not claim myself as a poet for another thirty-five years, it was his wondrous defining of place and character, combined with mystery, an edge of darkness, and music, that settled somewhere in my heart and waited.

∾

I have been told that poems whose subject is the domestic life too easily become sentimental, unimportant, and cannot rival the value of the great themes of war, death, loss, and love. I have been told that the poems of family and motherhood are as essential as water, subjects needed by every mother, father, son, and daughter. I have come to believe the latter—to know such poems as essential, and that every traditional poetic theme runs through them like blood.

~

These are my necessary poems. In several ways, the writing of them saved my life. Saved, as a record or history documents a period of time. Saved, as helping me to endure and enjoy my daughters' young and adolescent years without being overwhelmed by a sense of entrapment. Saved me, by providing a vehicle through which I learned to balance motherhood and marriage with my identities as woman, writer, and teacher.

~

The earth cracked around the bases of trees and crocuses broke through. Ice shrank away from the lakeshore and the sky was that low gray New Englanders live with much of the year. That last afternoon with my father, he sat with me. I held a yellow legal pad on which I transcribed his thoughts for the last chapters of the novel he'd been feverishly writing and sharing with his family since the coinciding of retirement and cancer. I promised to finish his work. My eyes filled. But I could not return to a novel about romance, medical school, and the influence of war on a young man's life. I have taken my inherited love of language, storytelling, and imagination to poetry.

~

As much as poems are story, this book is a chapter in mine; and yet the speakers of many of these poems are interchangeable. I find my girlhood intertwined with my daughters', my marriage confused with my parents', my aging entangled with my mother's, my voice melding with voices of women I have known and others I know only through their written words. This is the delight in making poems. One makes discoveries. One becomes more intimate with one's own life. One absorbs and gathers rhythms and images in unexpected combinations. The poet feels previously unimagined things, has moments of clarity, collapses into tears in the writing. Assembling, recording, and revising are replete with mystery and surprise.

～

In this book, I have tried to orchestrate a journey. It is my journey, and perhaps it is the journey of others. I am indebted to many writers who traveled before me. To Adrienne Rich, Alicia Ostriker, Tillie Olson, Sharon Olds, and Rita Dove, to name a few, I owe thanks for paving the way. I am thrilled to have set out on the adventure of making poems. It has been the richest and most satisfying of any in my life. Thank you for sharing it.

—Barbara Rockman
Santa Fe, New Mexico
2011

I

SOLSTICE

She is happy her father has come without excuse.
Against glowing moths and Milky Way, they collect
flashlight, matchbook, the box of fireworks.
And since he is happy, they sing and arrange
cardboard tubes, volcanoes named *jade garden,*
butterfly burst, stairs to heaven
in the middle of the gravel drive—silver
and orange fountains repeat and fizzle.
The girl hops and gasps. She has both parents
to herself, for her mother has come away
from the house and dances in dark circles,
waving sparklers from each hand, looping
light, but who can follow wild cursive
she inscribes on sky, of love that flickers
and falls in this longest lit night,
letters that will not be sealed
and sent, but burnt beneath flesh
forever as *happiness* in the girl's long life.

PHOTOGRAPH OF THE IMAGINARY DOG

For days the weathered picnic table had been tipped
as puppet stage for her one-girl shows.
Posing in front of its rough wood,
bandaged knees in focus,
curls sweat-pressed,
she whispered *Sit*,
commanded *Stay*,
and the flop-eared stray
must have obeyed;
the string leash,
loose and weighted,
faded out of the lens
into which she smiled.
But her eyes looked off
toward the restless dog.
Good boy, she whispered,
Stay, through the camera's click.

BODILY LOCATION

Shoreless insomniac, crone
with no cause, I lose pages of my history.
My body is echo but not hymn. I give in—

>   horse chestnuts peeled to the mahogany nut,
>   island of milkweed, holes dug deep
>   like bunkers we kids could turn into homes
>   roofed with broken boards. Pretend,
>   pretend to be enemy, settler, doe.
>   Those big, slow days.

Is it rapid-fire radio drilling
sex and purchase
that terrifies my daughters?
Or teen girls, madonna and bitch,
black-edged purple lips,
their boyfriends' T-shirts
dripping crucifixions?

One daughter's song scrapes high notes,
while her sister writes existential lyrics.
Bodies of missed beats—

>   oh, my childhood town, shopkeepers
>   who knew my name. Anonymous
>   nickel and dime, stolen lipstick called Peachy Keen,
>   black and white photo, four faces, crammed grins
>   and grimaces.
>   Round and round we spun on chrome stools wanting to
>   get dizzy.

in each paper cell

        emptiness
gray light chambered
symmetry that astounded.
The firs breathed overhead.
As a girl I'd overheard stories
                 of sting and nest

how I could take weightlessness
in my hands and understand a swarm
that had abandoned
harm that could be done
           wings and vanished wing . . .

Underfoot   crunch and collision
        cone boot dried leaf
             a sheen of ice
above   clouds like snow-swayed tents.

I believed

that because I witnessed
their stab and glitter   the stars
would repeat themselves
that everyone saw what I saw
that night's heaps of dark cloud
was relief
that God made it   that it was good
that with my head tilted skyward
I could turn my neck in all directions
my neck an owl's neck
the night sky was an owl sky
it was my sky
that there was no god
that the pounding
within my flat chest was god
that I could ride the owl's back
into clouds   my whole lithe body
wrapped around a white bird
in the magic   in the tall tale
in the longest night   in the daddy who told
the tall tale   in happy ending and good luck
that I would return home unharmed
stars stuck in my curls
lying under the cool clean story

SNOWED IN

Barefoot, buttoned in flannel,
    nose to glass, I would watch drifts
        crest windows, pasture swept of cows,

and, though I dreamt myself white-booted,
    tasseled, in blue satin, my baton a silver arc,
        the cheers, oh, to be high-stepping—

snow quelled high pines as pre-dawn
    radio listed closings, sweet aria
    of my entering iced feather.

Brittle rose bushes disappeared
    until the walk was a rift of white pleats
        on which stood one crow.

I WAS THE POET'S DAUGHTER

Your father is
down the hall across the blue
carpet   snapping the dish towel
at someone not you   telling his day
and joking with someone not you who
washes while he dries who not you laughs
at his pun so you
girl down the hall at your desk
are freed of his hovering
behind your chair   his replacing
yours with his big words
offering details about astronauts
or birds or presidents
but for now his ideas are
in the kitchen
with your mother
pick up your pen
look out to the musty
olive trees that after years
of your witness almost block
the view   take clean paper
he is in the kitchen with his new
his excited word   nowhere
to be heard
your mother in his arms
by the empty percolator
the smudged chrome toaster
by the stack of plates he has
polished and will soon put away
his sleeves rolled to that work
the wild clamoring down into
language   yours.

There is the thing I want to touch

    glaze of the black plate

    iced lake   the damp within
    an infant's fist   open shut

    where fingers play in blue heat
    over a girl's dark braids   and there—

    fine hairs above a woman's lip
        lit by a spray of sun—

I turn away

    console myself with rolling
    socks into black and white knots.

The wind has come up.
    I watch

    the back of my hand divides into
    known   not known

  my fingers poised

    above the patina of each day
    awaiting a pulse or—

        what is meant to hold me

        up to the light.

DAILY BREAD

I remember my father wrapping my mother
in his arms by the sink as if this was the cool drink
he'd wanted all day, how she didn't want the kids to see.
She'd give him her lips, but her arms stayed,
one hand on the rim of dishwater, the other
clutched her apron.
A friend is dying
the way my father did,
the same decayed appetite, pain
but the remaining will
to work at what he loved. Day after day he
brought his body to the novel he believed in,
the same way a friend hefts the flat of seedlings
he insists on planting, and the French teacher
plans the student trip to chateau country
even as the verb for death conjugates itself
in his flesh. We don't want to walk
this narrowing trail.
When my husband's stroke
froze his vision, his hand limp,
I noticed my sight weaken.
My hand could hardly grip the fork
and the morning paper blurred.
And my husband,
who would not recognize himself for weeks,
wanted simply to grip the box scores
for the World Series of that fall.
Valentine's Day,
and the rosy, snow-limned peaks I see
after snatching rolled news from the street
arch so like hearts, I believe

some god continues to remind us—
the morning's buttered toast,
whine and drum of girls' complaint,
my family's backing down the drive—
none of it certain. My bare feet bouncing
off cold concrete, the dog yelps,
and I'm waving, robe untied,
blowing kisses, both arms
flying from my sides

PREMONITION

The nature poet convinced us she inspires
others to roll naked in leaf rot, though housewives
I know deny a universe beyond the fenced yard

where I study weighted apple boughs'
bend-without-snap. Would-be bushels
press against grass as if they ask

Can you love too much? Oh, be still, head, rest
with this ripened fruit. Today I read, Search &
Rescue is trained to walk each unmarked trail.

Let them memorize every possible loss.

MOTHERHOOD

If the Chinese doctors are right,
my moonless nails define absence
of spirit. I will grieve as they advise—

if only my hands had not been stolen,
if my fingernails cradled cuticle moons
like the dolphin's horn at sea,

if my blood had not been leached
by those darling deadweights who knocked fists
at my bone walls and fired BBs at the flying

saucer moon. *Let us out*, wail the buried slivers of light
beneath my flesh, while those noons and dusks
with their bawdy songs and hands meant to set fire to
underbrush,

take my fingers like sugar tits and suck
the curve of night. If only I had been warned;
if only I had worn white gloves.

BROODING

My daughter dyes her hair blue and sports
a peace symbol tattoo on her flat stomach.
The younger one grows dreadlocks and does not bathe
in her sister's religion of self-attainment.

It is suburbia, so there is their Dad,
like the miniature trainman on his Lionel set,
going in and out of the station
on the same half-circle path,

raising and lowering a warning signal,
and though the fated season is over,
our fridge is embossed with Cal Ripken's grin,
a man who "just got up and went to work."

Faced with the sink of orange pulp and oatmeal,
I long to shave my head and pierce my lip
with a diamond stud, but make do with a trim.
Watch Road Runner chase Coyote for dear life.

The day's backwards within glass channels that suction
my children's morning like a syringe of time.
Outside, the yard fills with rusting bikes
and collapsed pipes of a swing set.

The tinted daughter defines herself by the lit
mall map that says *You are here*. But at night
she discusses god and afterlife, tells me
we all have a lesson to teach,
we just don't know it yet.

LAUNDRY

The wife has dismissed his long-armed words,
gagged on her own gossip, gone to the blameless
laundry. Socks wag like tongues pinned
to rope strung between two trees, wet towels
hang like old ballads. Ask her how it feels
to loose the tongue from its trunk of wool
and mothballs. Watch her stretch in the arc
of his shirt billowed behind her:
sleeves without hands wave over her,
fill and fall, fill and fall, while she follows
a flight of jays. Air so lean and quick
she's startled by its heat on her cheek.
Her breath, her breasts crest like hymns.
Red leaves congregate in white sheets.
She stands within the canopy of laundry,
her arms circling like propellers
until she ascends—
a stray pillowcase
pumped full by a gust,
easily mistaken for cloud.

GLOW AGAINST STONE

Watching the squat candle against cold tile,
the woman afloat in her bath imagines porthole,
glass collapsed from arched window,

eclipsed moon, mirrored orb over the dance floor,
the infant fist unclenched,
the missing doorknob.

She wants to unlatch the brass catch and
pass through the aperture she conjures in wax
pooling beneath the wick like a soft circle of flesh—

baths women go to
to hear the door click behind, to loose flesh
and hair like cut flowers freed from twine.

She floats and follows the slim prism
of flame, durable as rope
that hauls the bucket up from black water.

BONDS

She rubs her soft, slim belly and eyes me.
End of summer, after her 14th birthday, salt
and chlorine a vague memory: she needs
my permission to go to the parlor.

I imagine a den of tattooed gypsies, incense,
house musty with music by The Doors, everyone
bent under low ceilings and slow fans. There,
she will bare the belly once knotted to mine,

where I watched our blood
harden into a scarab until it fell,
and was lost, as I am, losing her
to a kind of beauty foreign to mine. A stranger

will force a gold ring through the upper lip
of her navel. Never again will I nuzzle
the crevice where, for years, I blew kisses
into the valley of the first land
created, the one time I was God.

CUSP OF SUMMER

Vines will collapse
and the leaves lament.
The bowed willow will
narrow its dream, forgetting
the June night a thousand ladybugs
clung to its undulant limbs. Gold
chamisa will throng with wasp
and butterfly. The window
of stars and breeze will fall
to a slit of moonlit cloud—
as if night were the season
we leave, flesh never
satisfied with her
unfurled days.

AS I WATCH, MY HUSBAND

abandons the baseball wrap-up,
goes out to gather fruit.
From the screen door
I watch
as he tosses
pocked and swollen
coppered apples to cardboard.
I hear them thump one on another.
He hauls collapsing cartons,
windfall rank with flies,
to compost.
Returning,
he pauses to hear late birds, then
reaches and snaps one tight fruit,
bites, discards, and climbs.
Braced by crossed limbs,
he pitches hard balls
into the night.

LAST HAVOC OF COLOR

I wake with *wreckage* on my lips
and my body like wet snow, no, caught
in deep drifts in which my knees lock;
arms paddling air thick with fog.

It's a season of fugitives, everything
giving up splendor.

My eyes fill at the mention of prayer,
at fallen peaches split with ants,
a lost-and-found friend who wants
to try again, and the surprise of rain.

In the desert, the last havoc of color turns
scrub jays directionless, can't get enough
piñon nut and berry, dart and covet.

Do we hoard what we're afraid of—
stripped trees, emptied nest, heart
a drawer full of ash?

II

TWO BY TWO

Two days before the snow came
in its even-numbered steadiness,
the animals showed themselves

as if to Noah, but without the required pleading.
Coyotes in mangy coats and splayed legs
loped across the last god-given space

between houses, and wolves followed
at night, gray shimmer and broad paws;
while all day the ravens rose

from usual competitions, counting off by twos
to separate perches; roadrunners, plumped
against wind, hopped their *quick-rush-*

stop-and-query and nuthatches
clung to the olive's bark, while inside,
in odd numbers, the humans did not

go out but watched from lengths
of glass, through telescoping lenses:
the man and woman, the child begot

by them, passed binoculars and stories—
once the mother had followed howling at dawn;
once he'd locked stares with the fox; while the child

claimed conversation with an uncommon
white bird on the roof—and momentarily,
for each rending of peace is brief,

they were tired, happy as if
hunted and then spared, and still
the coming storm.

ELECTION SEASON WITH RAVENS

In a land of no curfew, spare change
and borrowed beer, teens aim headlights
into the *not-so-long-ago* playground
of silver slides. Empty swings,
overseen by one raven, tempt them
back to the slipfast child night.

But they've inherited their parents'
jangled nerves and wrong agenda:
the heartland's candles
burn at both ends . . .

Fixed behind steamed windows,
they redefine *abandon* and *flight*,
ignite glass pipes and exhale
what the hell.

Later, home, hems of their jeans singed by sex,
girls twist into bedsheets and bad dreams;
boys collapse, clothed and unquenched
against sweat-stained pillows.

The moon fades to Sabbath—
the pews full of voters, polls full of hymnals,
a weary electorate prays for rapture,
for pumpkin rot to be washed
from the streets, to obliterate graffiti,
for the children to wake unscathed,

prays beneath a circle of wings
beating like bellows huffing,
   heaven sent
      directionless . . .

CONDITIONAL LOVE STORY

If snow's steady fall was conversation
if morning dug in her heels
if the barn   shimmer and icicle
if desire sprung from her stall
    sprawled by the bed
if the man sleeping beside her spoke
    the truth be known
if he   if she   if snow ceased
if need stepped up to the broken gate
    the trees moved closer   the man leaned in
if she listened with every limb
if the door flew open
she took his hand   if she ran
and snow clung to their hair
if the meadow rose to meet them
if they fell into its folds
    rolled under the fence
        fallen elm and oak
if the door swung shut
if no one saw   if they laughed
if he slept on   if she rose
if snow turned the other cheek
if they chose someone else

If the mold broke
if spring
if he said   if she
    a warm wind borrowed his name
if the shutters snapped   the ransacked barn
    hours but not years   onto death
if it came to nothing

if it surpassed their wildest fear
if he withheld   if she stole   if it went on like this
burnt toast   good news   sour milk   if flowers
   re-bloomed that were not meant to
if she could speak French
if he could read music   danger
   removed its mask
if boots piled at the door
if the man stripped and sobbed
if she held him
if *forgive but not forget*
if it was   not too late   if
imperfection's net stretched   if
ever after refrained from humming
if in time love

weeping is to pearl
as flight to calculus

the breeze-filled willow is   to the bent and dwarfed pine

what the coal-sheeted sky is   to the woman behind the screen door

what flooded banks are   to her dry cheek

gray-headed birds
flock the berried juniper
their blue bodies:

as calculus gouged from rock
as the pearl unlocked from its salt seal
as the tree's arthritic reach for sky

why does the bird nest in view of predators?
why does she choose the silent lover?

we scrutinize the bare field for trespassers
the car for dents   the lover for the wrong word:
we make of rapture its opposite

intrusion   yet the pearl
eloquent gnarl   from the twisted trunk
weeping's sweet allowance   the lover's soft step
storm-tendered sky: return these to the fragile equation

AFTER NIGHTMARE

choose the dream
in which an old lover lies close
shapes his palm to your cheek

such tenderness you wake
all day refuse to wash your face

tirades of the cruel
conscience have fled
the day lovely   you

want to name it
living with doubt
forgiving   which is what you do

surrender
to kindness

that opens your hand
to cheek brow now
cups your chin

into loving
the dubious   dangling
day   the self

HARANGUE

I said *harangue* in naming our daughters' pleading
and he nailed the word on the door
to proclaim his sentence:
living among women.

Keys and spare change that jangled
inside that word went unclaimed
and sounded like Istanbul's buses—
amplified laments of lost love,
scrabble of caged hens on women's laps,
the brakes' screech and grasp for solid ground.

Argument and complaint
twanged rubber bands our girls
stretched across empty boxes
and reminded me of everything cheap ever fallen for—
bonus flashlights that never shone, the bargain
blouse, its buttons robbed by the wash,
a lover who slept with my best friend.

Between our voices that blamed
spoiled children and each other, the word,
gathering of warriors; blustering tirade,
nestled insults in slingshots—

when the din settled and he left the room,
our neighbor's annoying chimes
were suddenly musical. I thought
harangue could name a new poetic form—
and, like white space at its beginning
and end, I was silent a long time.

FIRST NIGHT WITH BRACES

Where molar and cuspid, moonlit,
are thrown like Hansel's
white stones, to find the way home—
her sobs break my dream.

Since her dad's soft words fail,
I stand at her door—
Ice, I snap, *Suck ice.*
Cold stops swelling.

Certain I have
already numbed
my breast. Mother
of the armored heart,
I back into sleep as
my husband cracks trays,
releases cubes to tin cup,
and soon returns
to cooled sheets.

Silence,
then bitten ice,
like buckshot,
spit back to metal.

EARLY GRIEF

Maybe it's the movie he and I saw—the good doctor
burying his son's murderer in the Maine woods,
his retreat delayed by the bridge

ratcheted open, turn by turn, gaping like hands
moving toward prayer.

It is a good thing
to grieve early, to let sorrow shimmer
a path so we are packed and walking

when death strikes. Metal on metal, which is
what woke him, made the dog circle and collapse.
Though it was my cough, still he surveyed

the forest he'd been lost in,
its copper branches that click and catch,
and what hard fruit they bear falling like cannon balls.

The ground a frozen bridge bed,
his stumbling over abandoned armor
and broken microscopes—

I know he is helpless against his dream,
pacing for weeks the same acre
like a fenced beast. Hard rhythm of it—

anvil of his forehead.
And nothing I can do except say
I coughed

and offer my palm to his cheek
after months of circling grief's
dark orchard.

When his mother's death arrives it will be
ice split and slid into black water,
bridge hinges and surface realigned,
ready for traffic.

SEARCHING FAITH

After Beth and I choose,
for me, the lark fetish for its song,
for her, the silver necklace for beauty,
I watch the moon rise pierced by ridge pine,

and the shape reminds me how the Zuni
transformed the cross into dragonfly
and, hung from silver chains,
it is as if its wings are oars held out
from the stilled boat of the heart.

You can hear the slowing of water,
absence of the suffering crucifix—
how we shape another's emblem to our need.

My Jewish daughter stares straight, face blank
as the New Mexican night, *I might convert.*
She practices fingers to forehead and chest,
likes holy water, Hell . . . what do I know?

I want my daughter, whose name means house,
to find her way. At the intersection,
by church toward home,
turn signal ticking, hunger rumbling,
radio rap extolling the dark,

I point, *The moon!*
as if she might miss it,
as if it were that simple
and this our only chance—

COTTAGE, MID-SEASON

Blue bear and blue mist,
    the spirea swells with bees.
The sky like a javelin pitch,
    clear cut and diamond faceted.
Ripening & kind,
        out of debt & grateful,
not adjectives I'd have expected.

Heat sedates me,
    and middle age.
My daughters return from countries
    I've not visited. Twin hawks
deflect pewter &
    pearl-rimmed clouds.
Where is God in all this?
    Old question, ineffable lack—

foul smell under the back deck.
    On the front porch, God
in the old cane rocker,
    slouched shoulders, humble-eyed,
        waits for Resentment to collect his
dirty clothes and hit the road,
    to force his bitch, Envy,
who's made a real mess of the place,
    to pack her bags.

    Where am I in the pastoral tableau?
        Staring out the warped screen door,
    summer of uninvited guests—
        the ones I wish had come I never asked.

MORNING WALK AFTER STORM

Purple sage buds beaten by rain
stain the mother shadow.

What is the purpose of washing
one handful of cherries?

I fill letters to my daughters
with pressed flowers.

I rest on their smooth beds,
dream in one room, then the next.

Rain from the roof
overflows one bucket, then another.

IN SLEEP FILM

Two black horses in the neighbor's front yard.
Two whelps with watery eyes held out to be toweled.

Heartbrood. Rock salt. Daily deliverance from dream
into hard corners and the milky runoff of animal love . . .

On the street a boy walks his dog. On the highway
a coyote scans a break in traffic.

The dream paired animals like arguments, waited
for me to pronounce right or wrong.

What great spiritual teachers have done is—

The gray reel crumbles to broken bark.
                              It's not some faith

one can sweep into a cupped palm—

I choose the horses' silhouettes as my
waiting, and mine the pups' refusal

to die. Dim morning and there I am, back
in the kingdom of things: sour breath, red click.

Splayed book. Mid-sentence, digital, lit.

RETRIEVAL

If the roof of this house lifted,
what would be witnessed—

a man and woman of long-standing vows
who stare at tightly made beds, talk to the dog,
read the paper in a chair warmed by the other.

Looking out to their hedged yard,
they finger detritus in deep pockets,
hunt for some smooth thing

a bottle cap   folded note   a shell
that will remind them how they got here.
She finds the child's pebble   ball of thread

mottled button   crushed bud   recalls the climb
his hair plastered by rain   their weaving up
among aspens into pine

while he retrieves   his creased list
coins for the children   split feather
remembers birds scattering   the trail

narrowing   sweat   his falling into her body.
A hot breeze raises curtains
turning   turning back

turning the knob from news to concerto
they move toward the made thing that marriage is,
the smooth, long unbroken bed.

THE GOOD CRY, THE ROOM, THE DREAM

How clean the room is after a good fight
or torrent of tears, the walls holding
a rippling scrim of filtered sun.

The room, backdrop to fists' clench and release,
flat white, lusterless, is now cumulus
and incantation;

so that here in the slit-eyed morning
I consider dream's slim information:

silver fish line, I almost tossed
back, unwinding from sky to water,
its slippery wrap round my wrist so my fist
falls open like a sleeping child's
while the lit thread curls and shrinks

so I think what it means
is: the moment seized, the heart given time,
the eye, in due course, finding beauty.

The night's argument faded,
I see soft limbs beckon
from behind the lit scrim.

And then my wrist is caught
by a drift of broken filament,
bracelet of light, and I write

How clean the room is after a good fight.

THE EMPTYING

Nothing as they left it: framed and hung,

gone, tables and their unread piles,

nothing to hold them down, all taken
by hands that chant *removal*, each syllable

a soliloquy of loss. The house bereft,

each closet filled with the swinging air

of empty hangers. The unlit stove,
its abandoned burners.

Where are the bright contents
of the glass vase, the circle of surface it filled?

And where the bed stood, now a rectangle

of used light; broken snores
darting for cover—

such swift erasure.

MISTED REVERIE

Sun Mountain socked in by fog.
The dogs sleep in, the crows on sabbatical.
Rain sways to old tunes I can't remember who sang,
or where I first heard them—

mother mixing meatloaf,
father refilling his pipe,
the tobacco tin I'd beg to bury my nose in,
no TV, not even radio news, the table set,
hi-fi playing low jazz. Soon we'd be called to supper,
my brother earphoned to his reel-to-reel world,
I detailing dreams in shoebox dioramas.
A smaller dog curled under that table.

Every family's odd dialect,
jokes and boiling points passed on.
When we go, the photos curl nameless,
dateless, the stories re-created like rumors
by our descendants. Lost translation,
wrong quotation: who will ask
what we were famous for,
which wry line was whose,
who will confuse our names?

A LIT DARK

It is the darkest day of the year.
Longing is my undoing, mid-life and later.

Child-memorized, carols revive.
Lampposts barber-poled with greens,
swag wreaths, red-bowed and, above it all,
snow shaking down, night glow . . .

New England's corsets
untied and I, girl loosed on twilight,

skated the frozen swamp muffled among
brush, stubble, leafless oak, brackish ice, black ice.
What mattered was the footwork, frozen cheeks
like ornaments the sun dropped.

Orange-lit, I bladed past stumps,
fallen trunk. Night's clean stare down
my neck. Hot throat and dry lips,
nothing will retrieve that body.

NIGHT MIRROR

In earshot
of lone dog and late song
of one misfit bird, in dark mirrors
and black panes, I grow old and aimless.
While the ones I love
breathe in and out of dreams,
roll on soft thighs,

cheek to cold glass,
I lean on child recollection—
how my feet curved to the earth,
walking field stubble, granite-bound,
skirting cow dung. Beneath barbed wire,
my stomach arched rough ground.

Moonlit, my body recovers
those low hills and Holsteins
like favored cousins, hay-sweet
milk barns, lowing, and stray
kittens buttoned into
my hay-twigged cardigan.

Meadow, mown and baled,
cut pith and spit of wildflowers,
those blowsy, unbothered summer nights.
No one knew my thoughts or whereabouts
or saw what I saw or
needed to ask.

BUDDHA IN THE BEGGING DOG

Having driven my child to school,
having brought coffee in a cracked mug
and placed toast on a blue plate, hair damp
and the day cold, I return to the rumpled bed
to read, write, to flirt with solitude. But
the dog's nose is a submarine's scope:
she begs the crust, which I toss, and open
my book. Her stare so unwavering
I am forced to choose
   to lose my inner gaze to hers,
   draw her presence to the empty page,
   command her, *Get,*
or wrestle her lonely bulk up among crumbs
and crumpled lines I'd only half-write
without such longing, such
pleading, such hot insistent
stinking breath.

III

CROSSING

From under the mother's skirt
the child steps up to the corner,
knee high and curious,
at last ungrasps the hand,
gazes down the block
at the whole world—
looks up to the mother's waist, her chin
like a ledge on which rests
anxious love
and the child shivers—
the thrill of the city,
the hill and slab, fume and grass of it—
as the mother's freed fingers
stretch in the agitated air;
familiar grip, gone,
looks down: nothing but
the youngster's laugh hung in her path—
she will cross the street now,
fixed on her own future.

IN THE CITY OF HEART

On the west side, Grief rents an office—
the door's dark wood frame suspended,
its smoked glass punched in
so ragged shards outline the sign
on its chain flipping
OPEN/CLOSED,
which is the way it is
for clients come to sit opposite
ghosts who counsel them.

The councilors of Heart pace and brood.
How difficult, they whisper among themselves,
to release the tenants from their lease,
to permit the blackened windows,
the stoop of crumpled handkerchiefs.

How eager the town fathers are to shuttle the bereft
to the sun-streaked sidewalk that heads east,
past the freshly painted gazebo, clipped
hedges and sprays of jonquils,
into the playground where children
slide no-hands and swing,
brushing earth just long enough
to propel the body to fly out
and over its wavering shadow.

TRAFFICKING IN THE IMPERFECT

Lovely, fallible earth
we criss-cross, redesign, and
to the eager pruners
leave behind—

the jowly man on his cell phone
balancing a burrito in traffic;
a carefully coiffed matron
in wraparound sunglasses,
blouse spread to tired cleavage;
and the crew-cut, tattooed boy
lightly thrumming the dash in
slouched recovery from sleep.

Windows tentatively scrolled down
as birds cluster May's makeshift heat.
Morning, like a white sheet spread, earth's
damp spots bleeding through—

I pass a woman bent
to trim an amber hedge,
her garden-gloved hands
itching to thin and synchronize,
as I, so often dissatisfied, believe
myself in need of shear, and simplify.

But even the tended lawn
turns mole-ridden and ridged,
shadowy turf—

JUNE

Must-brown and wings wide
   the moth floats on creamed coffee
Dark specks in the lemonade
   Lamps circled in gnat litter
Honeysuckle tilts to hum and flutter
   Demitassed buzz and sip
from waxed cactus blossoms
   June lifts and falls

fritillary and fecund
   Currant bushes nonpareilled
with aphid ant and ladybug
   Pine jays edge finch eggs out
Coyotes lope the arroyo
   Deer leap adobe walls
Bunchgrass bindweed blue flax
   June's squint-eyed and eclipsed

moon muffles the garden
   night sage and sanctuary
Gates latched against rabbits
   The wheelbarrow catches rain
On the back step tea steeps
   Windows streak wet dust
June windswept and sex-crazed

Prairie grasses gone mauve   wheat-
   gold and rust swing and settle
Un-cut-back yarrow live-wire and jazz-fed
   Tires crunch gravel Jewel-lit
days cool in the nick of time
   No one is hungry for meat
June strangles and releases

   hums *whole summer still to come*

CUTTING BACK AT 83

A crow's sharp call erased by
   the lapping
      re-lap lap re-lap.

My mother is bent into the hummock of garden
   overhanging shore. Snip. Gleam of clippers,
      spray caught in the water-dragged bushes.

The butterfly spreads wings like a tablecloth—
   while the water goes on weaving,
      undoing itself. *Braid, re-braid—*

clover and the bee lit in sun's tight angle,
   familiar lake cleared and raised
      after rain, more itself for its absences.

Next she attacks brambles behind the shed
   where oars and croquet are stored.
      Always, she's been busy while I dreamed.

Two crows glide.　Black ripple.　*Dash-silver-dash.*
   The day deciphers itself.
      Once, and again, we are the same body.

THE CLINGING

I want to press my hands around
the throbbing flanks of the robin
paused on the path.
My hands twitch
and beat their five-fingered
trembling hearts. I want the bird's heart
in mine to protect it from departure—
no, to stall my loneliness.
I can invite the wild thing
into my open palms. I cannot
expect willingness.

How she has suffered—
split claw, shattered wing,
stolen egg—
now she curls her exhausted
beaked face beneath her wing,
and her pulse becomes
lifted oars, drift
and no rowing.

Now.
Now, mold fingers to her
whole feathered body.
How glad I am to have her.
Held breath and songless,
breath and tremble—

how sudden
her whip and flapping,
her befuddled, urgent departure—

CLIPPED WINGS COLLECTED

(from the mixed-media installation, *Surrender to Storm*)

Before we scooped the beatless and big-eyed
winged things in our palms
and were reminded
  of brush and whir
we were soar and sleep simple
  even satisfied

Except for the worn beaks
and leftover sense of flutter
the bowls might be filled
  with gray gauze stitched with
    black stones honed to triangles.

Light rolls over and reconfigures
piles of tiny bodies   clipped wings.
We rename grief
  denial and refuge
    wreckage.

These discarded lives
are nature's refuse but lovely
  frail   in certain shadow
    cease to exist.

Emptied   rubbed smooth
the bowls are weathered cradles
  as if death could not happen here.

Oh   heart-stopped ones
fall and fall from the sills
from limbs from a thick sky
    into our rough-hewn hands.

MY PARENTS LOVING ART

Each artist they fell in love with
knew it was more about them than him
or her   how they'd return to the studio
inquire about his youth eager to know
where what they loved came from
and so they drove and stopped
pondered each possible acquisition
returned with low voices humming
each other's tone and taste until they
chose and purchased
that was the beginning
then   which wall   the light
what side of the curtain
how they'd comment
for weeks on subject and shape
the drape of line   the color
how the morning sun hit
how incandescent its mood
the artists knew
that afternoons in galleries
decisions made in white-walled
or paint-splattered rooms
were an excuse
through stroke and hue
to share imagined invention
echo revelation with a stranger
who somehow reflected
their ever shifting aesthetic
the quiet rebellion from the expected
love takes   so their house became

sanctuary and theater
of the avant-garde
the pastoral   the spare line
temple and inspiration
of hushed tones
and negotiations
that had drawn them closer
on the drive home
he'd spread his free hand over hers
radio on Copland or Clooney
refuge and renewal   one afternoon
makes of a marriage.

WHAT GRIEF ISN'T

My grief is not a lake
or ducks' arrival in mist
morning's slow glimmer
out of which sails rise
miniature and moonlike
It is not the dock
or the deep end from which
I am invited to dive into
cold springs or
flesh unready to be stunned
or the rough bottom
the feet too tender nor is it
the surface of sheen and glisten
the lustered air
mist of our undoing
off-lake and ambient   It is not
the old wooden swing's rope
splinter-ridden
to which we do not come
gloved or loose-gripped
nor is grief the hammock
unprepared for our weight
or the trees like arms held out
unfilled uphill from the riffled
shore which is neither sorrow nor night
Grief is not the sun flashing
the long-eyed glass house
or morning's soft focus
nor can the ducks floating out
to the lake's calm center

surrender to it nor
the boats' wakes
etched on
its reflection of low purple hills
define it as if the house
mirrored on the surface
will imprint itself
as if water is
impermeable and forever
as grief

AT WAR

Daily, the papers list death
and defeat and we hug
in the driveway, we hug
by the whistling kettle,
we hug mid-sentence and
sleeping beneath comfort
young soldiers have forgotten
in their terrible shaking dreams,
we shape our breathing,
our need; we hug however
we might shape peace.
We hug
fiercely and more often,
knuckles dug into
each other's spine,
ridge now littered
with frightened soldiers,
libraries' burnt texts,
with our leader's shameless grin,
temples and shrines
in the city of magic carpets
and hidden treasure
haloed by missile flame.

PRAYER FOR MY DAUGHTERS

That the world will not end
before you sleep in a high meadow
beside one who loves you,

the swish and rub of damp grass
and dew weighing the tent waking you
as you turn to morning's slow firing

with nothing but time.
That he will yawn,
draw you into his arms,

the awkwardness of down bags
and crunch of your natural mattress
not mattering, and not just the kiss

or the breeze rippling your luminous
blue house, but the zipped-in knowledge
that the bad coffee over the gas stove
and the oatmeal in tin bowls warming your hands,

the trail lined with larkspur and jays,
that even the lake you will reach
as the mist lifts, because you
are that eager,

are the beginning
and that one day you will return
and say, Once your dad and I slept . . .
but the children will barely notice the spot,

grass and wildflowers no longer flattened,
so fixed they will be on reaching the lake,
and may it be so.

DESPITE DARK MATTER, THE GIRL GOES FORTH

Despite the tightfisted and crass
in a land of surveillance,
there is a girl who,

despite tenants of culvert and cardboard,
walks available sidewalks
beneath an architecture

of embellishment—
late sun's orange boxes stacked,
wingflash etching brick stories.

Despite dark matter and tree-strangled kites,
she looks up—stars snap and unsnap,
fall from the sky's unzipped jacket.

Leaning into smooth bark,
she feels the glisten of skin,
abandons her city of few parks.

Despite dust,
swarms of flies, mud rut
and empty streambed

she follows the seekers'
bent shoulders and bowed ankles,
cotton sacks soft on their backs.

Shadowed by a dropped petal moon,
the girl walks as a charged air
rises around her.

Despite an energetic dark—
the falling, the breaking off,
showers of planetary light,

the pelting of stars, exquisite
whirl and sling of flame
and rock—she insists

a peeling of layers and melting,
darkness disrobed, the girl
spinning naked in her new night.

IV

SOON, MY MOTHER WILL DIE

The season is designed with dark letters.
Eaves guttered with wet leaves
and the rank wit fall offers.

Like her, slack skinned, it stretches
a thin hand over root-ridged paths,
to the lake which,

like a polished plate, waits
for decoration, for its edges
to be trellised with gold leaf and ash.

Lake of the last house,
motherless and unafraid,
luminous like her creased cheek.

Like leaves flattened to the soles of my shoes,
the imprint of her long walk presses into mine.
Maple-tinged sky, so clear it might be lying.

DRIVING THE HIGHWAY, I THINK ABOUT BEAUTY

The monarch opens and closes
its tessellated cape, faces my road-weary eye
    before it collides with the windshield's
    pretense of sky. Oh, if we could steer beauty's fate.

Once, on a trail fluid with moths—dozens
skewered by thistle, luminous wings'
    last heave and flutter—my breath
    was taken by life's elastic snap

back on itself. In the car, left with the butterfly's
torn smear, I think of a teen girl I know
    who designs her breasts with intricate crosscuts.
    Once lovely, broken flesh

exposed as now, bled and blackened,
    a doe's severed head
    by the side of the road.

Severed wing, broken body, and the girl
    walking away from herself.
    The remains, beauty's phantom.

COMPOSITION WITH BRASS AND WIND

What to name the rage and commotion—
I-25 Pink Sky at Night
splendor so raucous I wonder why

others in the line of rush-hour traffic
haven't pulled over
to take the shake of shrill color
to their overworked hearts

I am alone
      with the jazzed desert canvas—
            neon edging every piñon
        gold riff and crimson ridgetops
     flat roofs lifted as if lit for Christmas

      reverb so loud   thrill so obvious

but cars whiz by turning on headlights
bad news and ads' raised decibels
the sky screaming

Come-on-let's-dance
      pledging allegiance to surprise and spectacle
        foot-stomp   glory hallelujah
     enough voltage
        to jolt the whole tone-deaf world—

but the stream of taillights
snaps and twists into the distance
the gotta-get-dinner-on-the-table crowd

disappearing but one   replete and radiated   hawk

leans in and out of the lingering
        long whistle of a distant sax—
            dipping
                    steadying
                            heading home

work

you drink cool water from a glass
blown through with blue lines
while looking out at the day
after the night the oak exploded
in its gunshot hotshot riptide glory
its leaves waxed with a dye the color of blood
of heart of flame's high tender/tinder
you stand thinking you
are already at work
wanting to scratch words
about water and leaves
on a scrap of napkin
even as you let the dog out
you rekindle the dream in which you were
encircled by friends
in a house with wood heat
everything on whole wheat
sprouts and avocado
tomatoes juicing
Randy's beard then
a raven flashes the present window
you await his ritual roof pecking that pisses you off
you're at work so you pencil what it reminds you of
that peck peck click click
scrape of a hundred annoyances
friends and lovers
who needed too much
keys that had to be angled
jangled twisted and shoved to jimmy locks
to unjam doors you'd overshot/overshut
already noting you're overstating

what you should cut but
the kitchen faucet's stream
caught in sun as it fills the coffee pot
is the link and clasp
of this jeweled morning
which unwraps too fast
your stomach grumbling
dog wanting in
you pay attention
to her joy-wild roll and romp
ball toss pandemonium/living room havoc
of red rubber hurled against table leg
drawer pull   couch shoulder
flail and fuel of ecstasy a good shit
and coming in from the cold brings but
out of the corner of your eye still
the oak's glistening shimmy
you remember other oaks maples
birches from a long-ago landscape
and how as November robbed them of color
their brittle rasp and catch conjured
locks   wood smoke   broken love
and the damn raven's knocking
some prized (probably red) nut
on your flat roof right now
your work
to cull and twine
to make something
of this day barely begun

THE GLASS

Because overnight the surface froze

the water glass has become rink
to miniature skaters bent to circles
and figure eights. Imagine

a minuscule man, huddling

over the hole he's drilled,
his dropped line invisible,
rubbing gloved palms.

Tiny skiers come to glide

the pond's unswept edges.
Clouds sink so low, they fill
the glass with froth.

Below the iced divide

sediment swirls brief storms.
Lake weed shudders and folds
around divers who search

for the missing.

The man reels in his last fish
as the crystal disk spins past
the glass rim, up and out into morning—

eluding gravity's frosty grip,
the depleted life,
the half empty.

DAUGHTERS

When I became someone to slip past
down the dark
dangerous hallways
of their lives
when they lied to me
when my opinion
became nothing
when their breasts crested
bellies secretly pierced
and their bodies
fondled by strange boys
when they loved their bodies
in ways I'd never learned
they spoke in tongues and shunned
meals I set out   my jokes dumb
in bottom drawers   mysteries
I had not folded
when behind my back
they snickered and laid blame
I predicted pins stuck in a small doll
in my likeness   I stirred
in dreams   I paced their
post-curfew rooms
their rooms at noon while they
were schooled in revolt
every word   *root   nurture*
future   umbilicus   hip
became loneliness
where I had been target they
became arrows
where they had curled

against my body they shot from me
out of range   all the taming
and hovering   shredded
their shadows all
that remained in the dim-lit
once upon a time to which
so often summoned
I'd been a promise
their need a given thing
hearts engraved and silver-chained
have worn thin   my daughters
go without their given names

BEDTIME FAMILIAR

My bed busy with blue gasps
and sudden laughs,
my dead parents

unfold love letters
illustrated with stick figures
who smoke and tip top hats.

Her arms hung with cold hands,
like slow pendulums
rise and fall along my sides.

My mother's skin so thin
it could break against air,
wrists scratched

by the snapped stems
of plants she's deadheaded,
grass-stained dungarees

flapping lean legs
she wraps around mine.
I forget nothing, she says.

A joke on thin lips,
the metal box in which
his unfinished novel slumps

and the yellow pad scribbled
with possible endings
dropped at his side, my father

stretches beside me, freckled arms
propped on my pillow, his breath
smells of pipe, he tells a new story

but mid-sentence, beaming
the distracted grin of the dead,
he slips out to float above the lake,

thumbing his homemade
flipbook of dancers
in soft pajamas.

IN THE SEASON OF SUBTRACTION

If I prostrate myself on a bed
of bent reeds and leaf vellum
I will imprint upon, no,
the shore will imprint me. Bosque
of burnt letters and unfilled bowls.
The river runs its absent current.
Shoal of gilt pages, cracked earth
and a three-pronged twig.

In the synagogue, supplicants
yearning toward the Book of Life
lay themselves in carpeted aisles, forehead to floor.
While I press against autumn's heart, the cottonwood's
spade-shaped leaves flip and flail, caught in the cells of salt cedar.
How sad we might become in stillness.

Around my ankles, a strangle of dry grasses.
Around the fencepost, a twine of rust.
Along the river's edge, bird shadow but no song.

TO THE POET WHO REFUSES HIS SONG

As dry snow swirls, a roofer's drill
fills intervals of bird sound.

What gives the clear-throated
creature its insistence to be heard

despite bitter weather—
and how to interpret his mood?

As loneliness, *Come, gather.*
Warning, *Prepare, prepare.*

This is my acre, possessive,
and brassy, *Break away,*

twittering throng,
the morning is mine.

Or to celebrate,
Iced earth! See it gleam!

The song disappears,

returns, pitched higher,
a hammer hitting metal.

Perhaps he simply loves
clarity in arctic air.

His morning practice,
routine as flight and work,

his way of knowing he is
necessary to the brittle world.

TRACKING APRIL FROM THE TREADMILL

first robin   face front   still and steady
is a ripening pear   its upturned beak
the fruit's snapped stem

∾

a red jeep leaps road ruts
a jogger crisscrosses rail tracks
lone dog wags and sniffs
wild-scented unexpected
this and that

∾

I wait for the bone tree to bloom
backdrop to ever juniper and
sumac's ready candles
its bouquet of bent arms
tined with arthritic hands
without known history   future a mystery
first spring witnessing these bodies

∾

my left leg
is shorter than the right
despite how I stretch and
steady myself against railings
I may always be off balance

∾

moths stitch paisley shifts
clouds open fat lips to blue teeth
piñons tipped with ornamental bushtits

∾

quick-start   self-test   reset   age
incline   target heart

I am happiest half waking
breaking into day's landscape
image and opportunity

     ~

ears first
rabbits rise   two   then four
fur the color of scruff and weed
white rumps lift   pleased I
lean into an imagined hill

     ~

still I watch for the bone tree to bloom

     ~

left leg   slight and subtle handicap
what decides a body

     ~

the bone tree will never bloom

     ~

today   a cloud-squandered sky
the landscape keeps its secrets
one quivering chamisa
one fly tentacled to glass

     ~

change charts its own meandering

     ~

May   and it's evident
my mortal muscle
cinched and eager   is not
the only body I call mine

LATE PROMISE

Since crouched in the berried thickets
since hay bales were hoisted to make-believe
since the last dusk walk out of the sog swelter swamp
since the path trudged tugging the warped toboggan home

I have hardly rested

so much work there was to be done
to become one with the labeled and runged world
to be in hot pursuit   to not falter   to marry and raise offspring
to answer politely to vote correctly to do in moderation and be wise
I have hardly rested

and so since I am tired I choose

less and what's been forgotten
choose late walks cold and pink hued
risk my cheek to rough bark   to stay long enough
to stuff pockets with scraps stones nuts rubbed a slick sheen

I mean to hide out

in apple gnarl   elm island and log spoil
holes deep to fit into   snow piled to live in
high limbs to dangle from   on a bent-fendered
blue bike   breakneck   downhill   hands-off   singing

I mean to hide out

BY OUR HANDS

Maybe today nothing will happen.
No one will walk miles for water.
Nothing will move in factories
where guns are built or
where bread is sliced and bagged.
On tables cleared of night's debris
we will spread our hands—

Officials will close their doors
and stare into the past.
Desks piled with bills and
half-written novels will neither gather dust
nor quake in the cubicles of workers where
light falls across feet twisted around
the rungs of chairs.

Maybe today nothing will happen.
Children will sleep against each other's breath.
Fields will go unmowed and mail
sink unsorted in bins.
Electricity will fail and prayers
in mosque and temple,
physics experiments,
the building of bombs,
the weaving of bright cloth,
will cease. We will
study our hands,
every line and knuckle,
each cracked nail and stain,
meaning something.

WALKING BENEATH

tragic dawn   half-mast sun

three, five, and then six quail out of hiding
snow's brief toss & flounder
the man and his German shepherd—
regal and mute until spoken to
(I could not keep the quail to myself)
yet every fence restrained a wild dog
every curtain closed as I passed
blurring blue flicker of repeated news

the team of astronauts had scattered,
broken meteors over the President's
state already plagued
by a steady descent of dead pigeons

x's of contrails,
grief's wrung and twisted arms

for weeks the jay had hung strangled
in loops of her own making   storm-tossed twine
severed soprano   willow
become house of death

the quail twisted their crested heads
ready for predators   did they think
one pedestrian breathing into her feet
might hurt them? oh, how we might
save each other

before the quail slipped from hiding
hadn't they put aside their slim meal
seed and rain   exposed themselves as feast
amid threat   heap of tied and tangled
budding branches on the curb
resembled pussy willow
as I broke them
they became bouquet

the hope-broken sky grew radiant
a joy ride   hosanna sky   no one can steal
the soul's bud and flourish

even while announcing the dead
under the downpour of accusation
even as the mourners' torn black ribbons
overlapped within clouds

the quail jaywalked
the shepherd's inquisitive ears
rounded the corner   the silent master
nodded at my arms full of the discarded

find bounty   the day plead
unfold that which is folded
break something
once considered sacred

This book of poetry has been typeset in
Adobe Garamond Pro.
Garamond is the name given to a group of old-style serif
typefaces named after the punch-cutter Claude Garamond
(c. 1480–1561). Most of the Garamond faces are more closely
related to the work of a later punch-cutter, Jean Jannon.
A direct relationship between Garamond's letterforms and
contemporary type can be found in the Roman versions of the
typeface Adobe Garamond Pro.

Garamond's letterforms convey a sense of fluidity and
consistency. Some unique characteristics in his letters are
the small bowl of the a and the small eye of the e.
Long extenders and top serifs have a downward slope.

Garamond is considered to be among the most legible and
readable serif typefaces for use in print applications.
It has also been noted to be one of the most eco-friendly
major fonts when it comes to ink usage.

∽